AMBIGUOUS

Tom Adams

Smoking Page Productions

Printed edition:
Also available in multiple e-book formats.

Published by:
Unheard Voices
An imprint of The Endless Bookcase Ltd
Suite 14 STANTA Business Centre, 3 Soothouse Spring,
St Albans, Hertfordshire, AL3 6PF, UK.

More information can be found at:
www.unheard-voices.co.uk

ISBN: 978-1-917061-12-4

Ambiguous
Supported using public funding by the National Lottery
through Arts Council England

Front cover photograph of trees by Mabel Amber from Pixabay

Dedicated to my mum, Joyce Bridgman

With thanks and love for all you taught me

Rest in peace

About the Author

Hello, My Name Is Tom Adams. This Is My Story…

I'd Been Working All My Life As A Chef. But When The Pub I Worked In Closed Down, I Lost My Job. As A Result I Then Lost My Flat And Suddenly Became Homeless…

This Lasted Six Years. When The COVID-19 Lockdown Happened, Quite A Few Members Of My Family Sadly Passed Away…

Writing Poetry Really Helps To Cleanse My Depression! I've Chosen To Be Happy As I'm Done With Being Sad And Feeling Down! …That's Why I Write My "HAPPY POEMS".

Some Are About Saving The Earth…

Some Are About Falling In Love…

Others Are Happily Silly!

Enjoy!

Tom Adams
Smoking Pages Productions

Contents

AMBIGUOUS

WHAT CAN WE DO?

Decisive, decisions, providing provisions for everything that we choose!

First place has beckoned!...
...We can't lose a second!...
...Because now we've got nothing to lose!

Yet people don't care anymore; they just stop and stare!...
And that's what's making us confused!...
Can good things come in twos?
So "What Can We Do?"...

Because our beautiful earth is not amused!
For it to be so abused...

We must give it a chance to refuel everything that is just!

We should pay it more attention!

Instead of the things that we lust!

Yet it's your life too!... But we all want an earth that's blue!
So really, people...

WHAT CAN WE DO?

MY HEART

Right from the beginning and right from the start
You've kept all my emotions, singing pure love from my heart!
With such feelings that will never be torn apart
They emit a glow that can be seen from afar!

And when you see it you'll want to dance!
Absorbing the love off of me, you'll not need a second glance!
Just be steady on your feet as it may knock you off your stance!

But with love as deep as plant roots
You should tie up the laces on both your boots!

Because I wouldn't want you to fall
Unless it's in love with me
So we can have a ball!

And our emotions will be right off the chart

As you are my love and will always have...

MY HEART!

HOLDING BACK THE TEARS!

Listening to storytelling perks up your ears!
Some can be funny and deserving of a cheer!...
Others can be scary and give a lot of people a fear!...
But my one's quite a sad one!
I've been… "Holding Back the Tears!"

Everything I've lost! Yet I see things very clear!...
I try so very hard to stay out of second gear!...
My life's been burnt on all sides like a steak that has been seared!

But now I've found a peace of mind so now I have nothing left to fear!

So I guess I will just stay strong!

And keep on…

HOLDING BACK THE TEARS!

A HAPPY POEM!

I need to have a laugh!...
So I drink another half of a cup that's full of fun!
And laughter is here as it will be forever after as something has
begun!...

I get butterflies in my stomach as my humour weighs a tonne!

And hopefully by now all of your sadness knows that this
"Happy Poem" has won!...
So with the rising of the moon and the setting of the sun!...

Behold my "Happy Poem" that's the best!...
Shooting down any upsets found in the Wild Wild West!...
Because I think that smiles are the only thing you should be
showing!...
As we have planted all of the happiness seeds that we have
been sewing!
And I can see by your sadness that is now displaced. We are
skipping up every stair and all of the way with footsteps that
can't be traced!...
Then sad times will never be part of what we are knowing!...

So I say knickers to the bad times!

Here have...

A HAPPY POEM!

WHO?

Who are you?...
...Who was me?...

Who is someone you will never be?!

Who has the answer for all the pollution in the sea?
Who ever knew our seas would not be blue?
Who hasn't looked after our beautiful earth as much as they can do?...

Who has bitten off more than they can chew?
Who wants to help save our earth?

Who wants to be a part of a selfless crew?

Who are you?...
...Who was me?...

Who can we change to and be all we can be?

WHO?

HAPPY TO DOUBT HATE!

The world can be a strange place!
Especially when it's filled up with such a nasty hate!

Yet still I have faith for the fact that humanity can still escape!
To a more sane ethos where things can be just great!

And I know we cannot wait for a goal that's not suppressed!

Since lately at the moment our beautiful earth is not impressed!

So let's make it our trait!
To dance happy and just skate!

We can fill our plates with a love harmony if you can relate?

Then maybe… just maybe our vibes on this earth won't just vegetate!
I want us all to go back to a time when we could leave our front doors open including the garden gate!
That's why I think it's a good idea to be…

HAPPY TO DOUBT HATE!

DREAMING FAST!

Hot was the Friday so I took the canal path!
The morning was peaceful!
Tranquillity was at its task!...
Everybody was happy! Polite to them I was whilst strolling past!...
Happy in their ways
I didn't need to ask...
...But I chat anyways, and we had a lot of laughs!

With gentile riverside folk tying up boats with ropes whilst drinking coffee from a flask!...

You see it's the way of life on the waterways where fishermen cast!

I really love The Nomad Existence
Instead of city folk dwelling on the past!

And I'm sorry if you can't keep up with my mind as if it was tied to a ships mast!

So I guess you'll have to catch up with me especially when I'm...

DREAMING FAST!

TOO MANY CHIEFS!

For too many day's I've been feeling like this with nobody
knowing why I can't resist!
Whether good or bad they all come with a twist!
Like trying to help a friend just to get dismissed!
And for too many days I've been feeling like this!

Yet with so many criminals and so many thieves at what vital
point do we get our reliefs?

I don't care for religion!
I don't care for beliefs!

All I know is that there are too many soldiers and not enough
chiefs!

But if we want safer streets that should be better policed just so
our kids can be alright
All night and day in parks where they play.

We all want a better world starting today!

Just think of what we can achieve!
If we just perceive and believe!

That's why we need too many soldiers!
And...

TOO MANY CHIEFS!

A LOVE OF ADVENTURE!

To be delighted is an emotion easily found
To be excited has made you scream out loud
"A love of Adventure" has made your hear really proud!
And to sing out in pure joy is a beautiful sound!

Travelling the world to meet lovely people continues to be
allowed...
As the lockdown we've all been through has gone deep
underground!

Our medicine has arrived and we have all taken the cure! Now
we live much happier now for that I am sure!

From country to country from ship to shore!

The sands of time are deserving an encore!

Now we fly high in the skies wings spread out so we can soar!

Nothing in our lives will be the same as before as now

We have found...

A LOVE OF ADVENTURE!

FUTURE BEE'S !

I'm Sitting Here Dining In Amongst The Tree's..
The Sun Is Shining There Is A Slight Breeze!
Yet I Can't Help Myself from Thinking of
    All of Our.....
    ... "FUTURE BEE'S !"....

They're Bumbleley Busy !... Making Me Dizzy
   I'm Happy As they're All full of play!

They Wear All of Their Medal's from
   All of The Petal's They've Visited
On This fine Day !....

But As The Wind Picks Up !.. One Poor Little
Bee Has A Hic-Up!... And Get's Himself Stuck!
Yet This Guy's In Luck !... Like Hooking A
fairground Duck !...

   As Because Of The Pollen !...
  ...My Nose Get's Swollen !...
    ...And I Begin To SNEEZE !

I've Blown The Bee free!...

  Now He Is A Bee full of Glee !
I Saved Him from His little Bee Sieze !
But It's Okay !... As I Will Alway's
   Lookout for All of Our.....

  ... FUTURE BEE'S !

10

FUTURE BEES!

I'm sitting here dining in amongst the trees!
The sun is shining… There is a slight breeze!
Yet I can't help myself from thinking of
All of our FUTURE BEES!

They're bumblebee busy, making me dizzy!
I'm happy as they're all full of play!

They wear all of their medals from all of the petals they've
visited on…
This fine day!

But as the wind picks up… one poor little bee
Has a hiccup… and get himself stuck!
Like mud on a truck! But this guys in luck!
Like hooking a fairground duck!

As because of the pollen…
My nose gets swollen!

And I begin to sneeze!

I've blown the bee free!

Now he is a bee full of glee!
I saved him from his little bee seize!

But it's okay! As I will always look out for all of our…

FUTURE BEES!

THE CIRCLE OF LIFE

It Starts In The Hands Of A Careful Midwife!..... You Deserve A Cheer!... You're Born Into This World To Begin Your New Life!....... The Adventures You'll Have Will Make You Have Nothing To Fear!..... You Are Here!... You Grow So Strong That Our Beutiful Earth Is More Fruity Than A Fine WINE!...... Finding Out That You Become All You Can Be!... You Go To School And Meet Your... YIPPEE!... So New That The First Time!... YIP-YIP-YIPPEE!... Start A New Job In A New Company!... Start Your... Degree!... Get Your Can Be. And... As You Grow Older... You Become Bolder!... Learning New Time!... Turning Your Final Page!... And You're Reached It... With None Of Your Bank Account Can't Get Much Higher!... And You're Done All As You Retire!... You Couldn't Wait!! And God's You Because... The Pearly Gates As If You Don't Be Late!... New Version Of... THE CIRCLE OF LIFE!... And As You Did Who Great!... Stone Now You... Stupid Rage!... All You Did With The Incredible Ease... Of This With Your family To Cry On Anyone's... Reach Earth... family With Its Own family!... YIPPEE!... You Finally Reach... To Go On Holiday Is To Have It... your partner for Life! Another... And When You're An Adult!... You Go To Colledge And Get... Drink It All Of The... And... Exploring The World For... Going On... So New For... The World For... & Now That You Are Here... The Very Happy Wife!... Your Mum, Thanks To You Dad, The Husband, And Thanks To Your...

THE CIRCLE OF LIFE

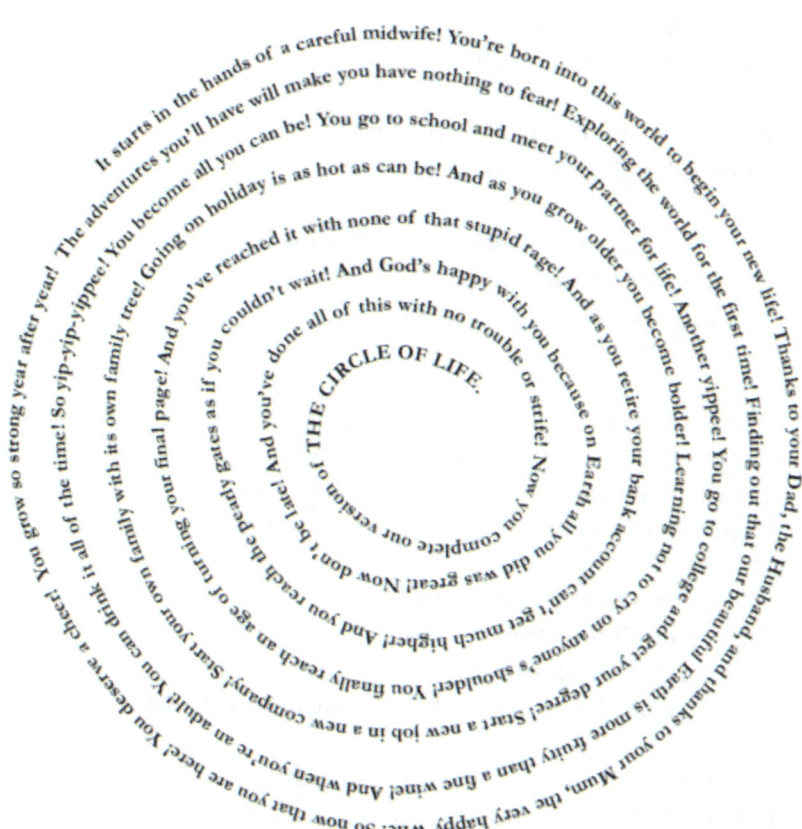

It starts in the hands of a careful midwife! You're born into this world to begin your new life! Thanks to your Dad, the Husband, and thanks to your Mum, the very happy Wife! So now that you are here! You deserve a cheer! You grow so strong year after year! The adventures you'll have will make you have nothing to fear! Exploring the world for the first time! Finding out that our beautiful Earth is more fruity than a fine wine! And when you're an adult! You can drink it all of the time! So yip-yip-yippee! You become all you can be! You go to school and meet your partner for life! Another yippee! You go to college and get your degree! Start a new job in a new company! Start your own family with its own family tree! Going on holiday is as hot as can be! And as you grow older you become bolder! Learning not to cry on anyone's shoulder! You finally reach an age of turning your final page! And you've reached it with none of that stupid rage! And you've done all of this with no trouble or strife! Now you complete our version of THE CIRCLE OF LIFE. And you reach the final bell! The pearly gates as if you couldn't wait! And God's happy with you because on Earth all you did was great! Now don't be late! Your bank account can't get much higher! And you retire your

13

RAIN!

Oh what a day!
Oh what a pain!

...Oh blimming hell!
...Here comes more rain!

But we are stuck here in ENGLAND
And nothing's going to change!

Wet pavements and water drops on plant leaves
Dripping down your neck!
Making you jump! ...and shout...
"WHAT THE HECK?!"

As the day goes on you get more wet!!!
But don't yet fret in your regret...
Try to rectify a hobby you need to find again!
If you don't you've only go yourself to blame!

So then you can for tell the future
That just isn't the same!
And when life gets all grey like
The skies of clouds that make any sunshine feel ashamed!!

Just remember all else is fine in England!
But you'll have to get used to all of the blimming...

RAIN!

THERE ONCE WAS THIS BLOKE!

Now we are all at this fun table!
Let me tell you a funny fable!
If you are able to get off your high horse and put it in
A stable!

So if you can handle… put your feet up and kick off your
sandals!
So I can continue to converse!
This world's a big place and puts smiles on your face! As if our
happiness is as big
As the universe!

Now low and behold, the stories are sold, as my poem business
has grown to be
Worth more than gold!!

Now I must invoke… A story that's spoke to many new and
old!
Like planet's and stars… we've travelled so far!
Through galaxies of fun kept in GODS funny little jar!
We pass by in a gaze, and shop in milky way systems for days!

Now we're happy we've had a great laugh!
We drive back in our cars, tipsy from bars, giggling all of the
way!
So with not much more to say
And we have laughed at all this poet's jokes
And so of course… Give a round of applause!!

Because…

THERE ONCE WAS THIS BLOKE!

A LOVE NEVER LOST

I met you for the first time way back in the day
Back when we had all of those great times, we played.
Together we shared fabulous memories, I remember them every
single day!

Our friendship was and still is so big that it will never go astray.
I'm so lucky to have a special friend,
In you, who I love, in every single way!

But as time and life moved on….
We drifted…
Yet our love never really went away!

I've been missing you too much to care
About this bill of love,
To worry what it costs!

Because deep down inside
We both know…
We have…

A LOVE NEVER LOST!

MY SWEET VALENTINE BLISS!

I can't believe that there are emotions like this!
On a crystal clear night
Not even the stars could miss.
Everything about you, I want to seal, with a kiss!

Let our entities entwine and be forever celestial blissed!

Because this kind of love never comes with a twist!
The ground shakes and moves many dunes in the desert, it
makes them drift!

As a love of ours will be the best yet to ever exist!

I'll give you sanctuary,
A home…
And all of the loving gifts!

So what do you say?

Will you be…

MY SWEET VALENTINE BLISS!

MOMENTS THAT LAST!

Enraged, encaged, enchanted, enhanced!

Selected, secluded, I've squandered my chance.
Insidious, incisions, fulfilling my past.

My dreams that I've dreamt!

My dreams that I've cast!

I welcome you into my world where we will be having the best
of laughs!

And we can spread the word of peace, love and joy to everyone
we pass.

Then even GOD can be satisfied we have done all his loving
tasks!

So we can fill the world right up
With so much happiness and harmony
That we create what's great about
All of these...

MOMENTS THAT LAST!

SOMETHING THAT I LACK!

There's something that I've lost!
And I want it back! When I can find it...
That will be that... Yet still the facts
Are in fact still in retract!
And I'm still looking for the one thing that I lack!

So I asked the postman as he delivered his letters!
But he told me that maybe there was no stamp on the back!

Then I asked a milkman as he supplied his bottles!
But he became angry!
And nearly gave me a throttle!
Then I was stressed and I needed a fag!
So I went to a newsagent to buy a smoke!
But he told me I need to buy so much more of which
Was a drag!

Then I bumped into a dog walker who was the town-talker
Yet it was her dog who nearly bit my back!

So now the facts are in fact still in retract
And still...
I'm looking for...

SOMETHING THAT I LACK!

STRAWBERRIES IN THE DRAIN!

It's a funny old life!
But I can't complain… yet something isn't right!
And I just can't explain…
I got this niggling feeling that's becoming…
A bit of a pain!

Since nothing I do works to try and save money!
And my life just stays the same!

I keep on tripping up every stair
But I guess I've only got myself to blame!

I wanted fame and fortune and fly far far
Away on a plane!

But it's hard to save! No matter how much I crave!

I need to break free from this bull
That's connected to my leg with
The heaviest chain

I want to taste a sweeter fruit!
Rather than these…

STRAWBERRIES IN THE DRAIN!

WOOH-YEAH!

I can't sit still!...
My boredom is ill!
My minds got a chill and my hearts got a thrill!

But even better yet!...
With my sadness dried up!
And my humours soaking wet!

Something in my shaky bones won't let me forget!

An energy inside has provided this great ride!

So these strong elastic bands can't flick away this feeling of surprise!

And with me off my chair and my hands up in the air!...
It won't matter if you stop and stare.

Because I have a moment of flair!

Now I'm skipping up every stair!

And I'm singing out "Hey Baby Baby!"

…"WHOOP – WHOOP!"…

WOOH – YEAH!

THIS TIME NEXT YEAR!!!

To have great ambition is born from…
A brainwave cheer!

To achieve a goal hard to score
Has made you feel you have nothing to fear…!
Trying to be first is only one stop above second gear
To get so far and be nowhere
Always' is so near!…
And when inspiration hits you
It will open your eyes so no need for your tears!

But don't think about it too hard on it may make your stomach
a bit queer!
Because a feeling of clarity is something we should all be
holding dear!
And when you get it right…
The bright lights in your head…
Start showing through the thickest of fogs and suddenly
everything becomes very clear!

Cash in your idea!…
…Show it off to others!…

…And just watch them sneer…
But all you should say to them is…

THIS TIME NEXT YEAR!

A SEAGULL CITY!

I really love being by the seaside!
The beautiful scenery
The cliffs, the beach, the smell of the sea air!

No way city life has any chance to compare!
Yet there is one thing that puts bad words through my lips…
Is when I'm eating my lunch on the go in the city
A greedy seagull just has to have a dip!

It swoops down stealing my lunch
Before I can even take my crunch leaving me shouting
"Thanks a bunch!"
Spilling sauce all down my top and that is a pity!

That is why I love the seaside!

Instead of living in…

A SEAGULL CITY!

POET TREE!

Can you not see?
I'm as happy as can be!
I'm the happy poet... By a happy tree!
Together we find all happy happenings

I've took my turn when everyone said my luck was a chance!
But now I'm spreading happiness out of every branch!
Tied up my laces on my boots so I don't lose my stance!
And when you're standing at the happy tree's roots
You'll just want to dance!

Even the squirrels have to take a second glance
Before they forget where they've put their nuts!

Because a crowd has gathered, coming from their houses, flats
and beach huts!

So as you can see we love the happy tree!
Everybody has had a great time and are full of glee!

Plus laughter is providing the sound of the ground
As a communal love is found!

And it's easy for me...
As I'm a poet and this is a tree!
Together we create happiness, joy and love

Because it's all just...

POET TREE!

STARBOUND!

In a dreamy sky, Night dreams can be seen
But never really found!
Shooting across the atmosphere creating magical sounds!
Sharing a love harmony even to the aliens
That have come around!
Even all of the planets, galaxies, moon's and nebula's have a
feeling that's no longer being down!

They've all come to see me!
As I'm making a loving universal sound!

Because my imagination is taking me far far away!
So I guess that I'm going to be a star!
And I will still be loving my family even when I'm somewhere
else and really afar!
Travelling the Milky Way I'm guessing I won't be needing my
car!
Since The God's! ... and the spirits in the sky have all agree that
I will succeed!
In anything I try!...
Because having ambition is something easily found!
And if you can't find it...
I can show you...
So you too can join me in my success!
Then we can all be lifted off of the ground...
So hopefully we can be...

STARBOUND!

A LIFE TO LOVE MORE!

I thought I was focused!
I thought I was sure!
Of living a perfect life!
One that was pure!

Maybe I'm ill?... Maybe I'm not right?
But the love medicine you're supplying keeps me up all of the
night

Keeping all of my dreams staying because
They are sustaining and definitely
Worth the flight!

A score worth to settle!...
A life to adore!

So surely by now I don't need much more!

My emotions are rising up to all of your
Loving floors!
To a penthouse of ambitions for all to explore!

But it's only you who I see!

As you make me feel like I have…

A LIFE TO LOVE MORE!

PERPETUAL LOVE!

Time ticks!... Time tocks!
Your heart strings are picking all of my locks!
From the moment I saw you… your amazing aura has knocked
off both my socks!

My emotions have become sweet music
That truly rocks!
And I know how we can show our love off
On every towns block!

Because the heavens above have supplied white does that take
true flight
Their wings are spread out so no need for a shove!

As I've met you now I've fallen in love!
Yet still I want more as it's never enough!
So I guess I'd better hurry up and put
A ring under your glove!...

Because I really cannot stop now!

As for you I will always have a …

PERPETUAL LOVE!

A HUNGER WHERE IT HURTS

I guess we won't be satisfied until
We have to leave this beautiful earth!

Because the days that we all live today is producing too much
pollution
And is doing more damage than it's worth!

Yet everybody that I see in my hometown
Just walks about oblivious to the reasons of my frown!
Too busy shopping for a mini-skirt or a wear once shirt!
I can't believe that they just don't care anymore!
And that's what really hurts!

I SIMPLY WANT THE BEST FOR US ALL!

As my heart has proved its girth

I really hope people change their ways
And walk one day in my life!

And have…

A HUNGER WHERE IT HURTS!

MY CLIMB!

What was I dreaming of in my wonderous mind?
What was I thinking of for a ponderous time?

Do I keep seeking?
Yet I'm led by the blind!
Do I keep searching for friends I can call mine!

Why am I tormented for being too kind?
Am I to stay alone with nobody to be stood beside?

Join me in my quest of bringing the best happiness to everyone
we find!

And together we can spread the word of peace, love and joy
And make God be pleased that we've made everything just fine!
So we would've filled The World Right Up with such a love
sublime!

Then I can finally put my mind at ease knowing that you've
Joined me in…

MY CLIMB!

ENDURE!

Enraged, Encaged, Encouraged and Sad!

Selected, Secluded, The Good and The Bad,
Involved, Excluded, The Slightly Deluded!
The Lies… The Truth… The Jury… The Proof!
The Rich, The Poor… We All Have to Walk Through Many
Doors!

My Hate, Your Late, Our Time that we had
And all of the times you've made me glad.

We Want a better world to explore!
And create many more better vibes that pick these in trouble up
off of the floor!

Our Loves, Our Lives, Our Kids, Our Wives!
Reasons we Cry, Reasons we Try!
And all of the Reasons we all sometimes have to ask God
"Why?"

Our problems, Our Troubles, Our Struggles…
Our Strives… Makes Us… Makes Us Feel
Alive! And "LEST WE FORGET!"
Those we've lost in The Wars!...
All are Good Enough Reasons
Why we must…

ENDURE!

CAN'T NOBODY BREAK MY STRIDE!

Can't nobody break my stride!
Can't nobody stop this ride!
Can't anybody find a better place to hide!
Can't anybody understand how much I've tried?
Can't anybody see my truth… yet only the lies!

Can't we just be happy and go to the seaside
Can't we stop all of the jealousy…
And just have pride!
Can't people accept the love of God and all
That he provides!
Can't we enjoy our lives that's still so full of surprise!
Can't things be better with no compromise?
Can't we just be happy without any demise?
Can't we get rid of all of the rubbish in our lives that just
attracts more flies
Can't my nights be longer so I can be dreaming
All of the time!
Can't I just fall in-love and find myself a bride?
And… I really cannot get much happier in life as…

CAN'T NOBODY BREAK MY STRIDE!

WHY?

Why do we do? Why do we cry?
Why do we don't? Why do we try?
Why do we jump? Why do we fly?

"WHY?" Is the question I'm asking "WHY?"
Why?... Why all of the years?!
Why all of the tears?
Why any disappointment? Why all of the fears?

Why so many steps?
Why so many gears?

Why not see more clear?
Why can't you hear?

Why not send me a letter starting with…"Dear?"

Why are all of your answers making my stomach feel queer?!

WHY DO WE DO? WHY DO I TRY?

Why is the question so please tell me…

WHY?

THIS!... FOR ME IS FUN!

I'm standing at the starting line waiting for the gun!
I get this feeling and I know I'm not dreaming when I think
that I've already won!
I'm not built for second!
Only for number one!

The race has not yet started!
So something can be done!
The other player's are all lined up under the hottest sun!
Some find it hard telling you "It can't be done!"
Others find it easy!
As sometimes it's easy for some!

We start with a BANG!

A shoelace goes TWANG!

All of the other racer's I pass easily
As all they do is just hang!
The race is nearly over but my luck in like a four leafed clover!

So the challenge is set!
Here!
In Somerset!
And...

THIS! FOR ME IS FUN!

THAT WAS THEN! THIS IS NOW!

Sometimes you have to have a break from the norm and switch
up your tradition!
Fed up of going astray in live and you change position!

But the world that we all now live in now
Has different rules and so there are
Many more terms and conditions!

So many try too hard to impress their neighbours
To "keep up with the Jones's"
Like its one big competition!

I guess that they wont ever worry about anything else!
Like the state of the earth's ozone layer as they've never ever
had the right tuition!

I really hope people change their ways and really start caring
about the pollution in our world!
But I guess that's all in fruition!
We should pay more attention to saving our beautiful planet so
God can say "Wow"!
Because…

THAT WAS THEN!... THIS IS NOW!

THE PURITY OF ROYALTY?

Everybody so say loves our country!!
Being so proud but not sure what to do with it!
This total disregard of the EFFORTS of those we have lost in
the wars
I am through with it!
Why can't we choose a morality that's not abused!

It's sad that people have forgotten
And are too busy being amused!
Kind of like the whole country has gone to sleep and is having
the longest snooze!
Fed up of Tony's society that's letting history get badly bruised
All need to change our ways
So our hearts have something good to prove!
To achieve a UNITED goal of remembrance and sanctuary of
our souls!
Take control… walk by poppies and have a stroll
As your peace of mind is there and that's a surety!
What we need is a monarchy who believes in more security, so
I am asking what's…

THE PURITY OF ROYALTY?

ZIP A DEE DOO DA
ZIP A DEE DAY...

Ha ha, He he, I love this way!

As the sun is shining and has his hat on
And I'm drunk with so much play!

How much do I love being this way with a whole lot of love for
us to feel we're on holiday!

Everyone is in the same dimension of joy!

And we all want to stay!

Since the summer is set...
Here in Somerset!

There's Not much more to crave!

But now that you're here enjoying our vibe

Your welcomed into our great hip band
As we continue to play!

A new song of ours, we sing
For hours! And It's called...

ZIP A DEE DOO DA ZIP A DEE DAY ...

UNDER THE MISTLETOE!

Christmas can be cold so wear both your gloves!
Christmas dreams of gold are brought by turtle doves!
Christmas can be flirty and make you fall in love!
But Christmas can be awkward
So give the snow in the driveway a real big shove!

And if you meet the reindeers then get on
The sleigh before they give it a tug!
And if you meet Santa Claus
Then give him a hug!
Yet when you're in the company of The Scrooge then just give
him a shrug!

The important thing to do at Christmas is to have a nice time!
Just make sure you leave for me some of that brandy wine!
And hopefully you'll be just as fruity and wanting to be mine!

Because I'm in love with your smile you have
Under your nose!

So pucker up gorgeous!
I'll see you…

UNDER THE MISTELTOE!

WALKING DIFFERENT PATHS

Tired of feeling bad, having better times always makes me glad!
And now I'm so clean because
I've took the longest bath!
So now let's have a laugh
Instead of the aftermath
I live my life so lean your won't cut it in half
We're walking different paths

And done all that was asked!

All the problems we've been facing and all what was tasked

Like we could be arsed!

We'll still have laughs that last!

It's up to you to change your ways
In another mould full of clay
That was cast!
And I'm sorry for the 'Fact that my mind' is 'FAST'
So you now know the score
As I said before we have to accept that were…

WALKING DIFFERENT PATHS!

WHEN?

When will it start?
When will it end?

When can I see your smile again?
When can I love your life you lend?
When can we be together and let our emotions blend?

When will it start?
When will it end?

When is the time when we don't have to pretend?
When will we get a new life and start a new trend?
When can we meet I hope this weekend

When will it start?
When will it end?

When can I call you on the other end?
When is a word I use in my text I send!

When will start?
When will it end?

When will you tell me so I can stop asking you…

WHEN!

SOMETHING BEFORE!

I'm ridiculed, I'm rugged, I'm righteous and raw!
I'm something now that I wasn't before!
And if you explore of what I've had to endure, then you'll be wanting
To know a little bit more!

I welcome you into my world where it
Is true and pure!
Then you feel a fantastic love right within your core!
So together we can bring the best love… And…
Happiness when we come knocking at your door!
To spread the word of peace, love and harmony
As future happiness deserves
An encore!
Swimming in paradise oceans, jumping off golden ships at the shore!
So now that you've joined me as we've now explored!

Hopefully you have become so much better than…

SOMETHING BEFORE!

THAT WAS THEN!... THIS IS NOW!

Sometimes you have to have a break
From the norm and switch up your tradition!
Fed up of going a stray in life and you
Change position...

But the world that we all now live in
Now has different rules and so many more terms and
conditions!

So many try too hard to impress their neighbours to "keep up
with the Jones's"
Like its on big competition!

I guess that they won't ever worry about
Anything else... Like the state of the earth's ozone layer as
they've
Never had the right tuition!

I really hope people change
Their ways and really
Start caring about the pollution in our world but
I guess that's all in fruition!

We should pay more attention to saving the planet so GOD can
Say "Wow"...
Because...

THAT WAS THEN! THEN IS NOW!

HA-HA-HEE-HEE-HO-HO!

Please stop asking about this challenge
I've been tasking, I'm tired of grafting for an amusement I'm not last in!

As you see when I show how my smile just grows, I think you should know
That my humours not slow!
I simply love life and I can't let go!
As my dreams are alive with
A BANG that can blow
Any roof, building or any café you may know
An erratic, ecstatic feeling too high
To be low, in spring, in summer
And even in snow…

I'm laughing all the way when I go home!
And if you can relate, I'm at my front gate
And tripping up in the garden on
A silly gnome, but I'm still not alone!
As my sadness is postponed, because Santa-Claus has come for brandy
When Christmas he owns, but its not
Just yet, so more drinks of regret have been sewn!
I tell him
To get back on his sleigh and say…

HA-HA-HEE-HEE-HO-HO!

BE MY VALENTINE!

You bring a feeling that I haven't felt for a while...
Every time I see you I look forward to seeing your smile!

The emotions you have made me explore I
Is something even all of heavens angels cannot ignore!

Because I'm confessing my burning love for you for that I am
sure!

You make me feel alive and with such an attraction
That even contest the strongest magnets
So they end up being insecure!

I can make our new love story a best seller
Being sold and told from ship to shore!
Because I know how much our love will shine
Until we grow old... I want you in my life
And I will have a love for you that's worth more than gold!

So now the story has been told!

With nothing less... I confess that my
Aim is to make your mine!

So what do you say? Will you...

BE MY VALENTINE!

TODAY'S DREAM

Sleeping in a doorway is as cold as ice cream
Trying to get a good nights kip
Hasn't turned out as easy
As it would BE seen!

Yet there is still hope for those
With TODAY'S DREAM!
When you're woken up with head lights that are stuck on high
beam!
Suddenly an idea of how the day should go and you become
very keen!

But you'll need some Dutch courage
And a few drinks later
You're needing a pee!
Then happiness takes over
And now you're full of glee!
And you can flick away bad energy
Quicker than any flea!

Meeting up with the right friends
Always creates "The Perfect Team!"
Which always helps to get rid
Of your nightmares
So you can concentrate on only…

TODAY'S DREAM

WHO EVER KNEW?

Forget yesterday!
I'm just through!
I'm stressing my mind so much…!

That my thoughts have
Turned blue!

Because the moment I saw you
I knew just what to do!

Try my best for your interest as
Who really ever knew?

The way that I feel is something
That is real!

The love I have held in my heart
All of my life you certainly did steal!

I need you in my life so we can create the heartthrob crew!

Because I don't know anyone
As selfless with their love
As much as you
So every time I look at you
An eternal love and…

WHO EVER KNEW?

OUR CRAZY WAYS!

Oh my days!
I really love our crazy ways!
Needing this amazing feeling to stay all day!
Now we both know how we can play!
In a night of fun… Now our friendship's begun
And nothing will get in our way!
So now we are bored! And we have run to endure
I'm not going to revert back to the chase…
As there's a
BANG!
From a happiness gun!

As this race is full of fun and still yet to be won
And with sadness displaced
And no disgrace we both know laughter is yet to become!
We help people we know, in spring summer and snow
Probably should not have taken off our clothes
And rolled about to the snow!
So don't yet fret if you are wet
As we can still glow!

To light all of our paths!
That's full of loving days! So we can love life.
The planet milky ways and even deep space!

But it's ok! When we wake up like this every day!
Because I'm pretty sure god love us. Even when
We are in…

OUR CRAZY WAYS!

SOMEONE I SHOULD KNOW

Not sure where to sit in?
Not sure where to go?
Not sure of my future?
Not sure I want to know?

Certain I'm believed in!
Certain I lead the show!

Obvious that I am followed!
Everywhere I go!

Depend on me to show you!
Depend on nothing you don't know!

Suspend all of the answers
That your suspending questions
Just won't show!

I can see you in the darkness of the night
When I watch your amazing aura in daylight
It shines with such an amazing glow!

In spring, summertime, autumn and even in snow
You bring such a clarity to me
I'm so glad that you are…

SOMEONE I SHOULD KNOW!

FRIEND'S WITH CLOWN'S!

The Whip's !... The Woo's ! The Up's !...
... The Down's !...

I Can't Help It !... I'm Always Going
To Be...
"FRIEND'S WITH CLOWN'S !"...

It's A Happiness They Bring When They
Come Around !...

A Symphony They Sing And I Just Love
Their Sound !...

A Melody That They've Put In The Air
And It Hang's About !..

A Chant Like A Plant That You've Put
In The Ground !...

You've Sewn It !....

.. You've Grown It !...

.. And Now You've Simply Done

Us All Proud !... Still I Am

Happy To Be......

... FRIEND'S WITH CLOWN'S !

BV - #0004 - 190624 - C1 - 216/138/4 - PB - 9781917061124 - Gloss Lamination